Punch *your* Art *out*

VOLUME 1

It all began last fall on one of those clear, crisp Colorado days.

We brought together artists Pam Klassen, Erica Pierovich, Joyce Feil and Tonya Jeppson to spend a long weekend surrounded by hundreds of punches and stacks of colorful paper. Morning gave way to evening and one day blended into the next as the artists punched, snipped and glued. Working as a group, they came up with ways to use punches they would not have thought up on their own. Out of those simple paper shapes, amazing ideas sprang to life, and hundreds of pieces of art were created. At the end of the productive weekend, we had enough ideas to fill not one, but two volumes! *Punch Your Art Out, Volume 1*, focuses on spring and autumn themes, while Volume 2 will feature summer and winter.

A lot has happened since that weekend, and we should have recognized early on that the book had a personality all its own. It demanded more from the artists, writers and production staff than we anticipated. It wanted to be bigger, better, more colorful and have lots of ideas. In the process of meeting these demands, we were almost forced to table the project. On the way back from a late-night photo shoot, my husband Ron was involved in a serious car accident. Thankfully, he was unharmed. You can just imagine the police questioning Ron. They weren't quite sure what to think of all the punch paraphernalia thrown around the van and scattered on the road.

In addition, as our artists looked forward to the birth of this book, Pam, Erica and Tonya all discovered they were pregnant. Despite morning sickness and fatigue, they continued to contribute fresh ideas and finalized designs.

And then…the big day finally came. Our labors of love culminated in our first book, and *Punch Your Art Out, Volume 1*, became a reality. We hope the projects within these pages inspire you to follow your own creative visions as you learn to punch your art out!

Michele Gerbrandt
Publisher

Special thanks

to Marlys Yutesler,

whose original work brought the

wonders of punch art to our attention.

Her ideas opened our eyes to the

possibilities of building with simple

punched shapes to create artwork

that is uniquely beautiful.

Art Direction Ron and Michele Gerbrandt

Artists Tonya Jeppson, Pam Klassen, Erica Pierovich

Writer and Editor Kerry Arquette

Cover Design Jeff Derkson

Production Designers Diane Gibbs, Susha Roberts

Contributing Artists Debbie Anderson
Carol Bussard, Rachel Cooke, Joyce Feil
Karen Gerbrandt, Nikki Patrick, Narda Poe

Contributing Editors Deborah Mock, Anne Wilbur

Photo Studio Jim Cambon

Copyright © 1998 Memory Makers Books
12365 Huron Street, Suite 500, Denver, CO 80234
1-800-254-2194

MEMORY MAKERS BOOKS

Originally published in book form by
Memory Makers Books, Denver, Colorado

06 05 04 03 02   7 6 5 4 3

ISBN 1-892127-00-8

Distributed to trade and art markets by
F & W Publications, Inc.
4700 East Galbraith Road, Cincinnati, OH 45236
Phone 1-800-289-0963

Memory Makers Books is the home of Memory Makers®—
a magazine dedicated to educating and
inspiring scrapbookers and paper artists.
To subscribe or for more information call 1-800-366-6465.

Gather up your punches, colored paper and some glue.

Heap a wicker basket full of sunshine, breeze and dew.

Throw in several smiles and some laughter you can share.

Then let your heart start singing,

'Cause you're going to a fair!

Punch Your Art Out

What Is Punch Art? 8

Punches 10

Paper & Adhesives 12

Tools & Tips 14

Basic Techniques 16

Additional Instructions/Sources 47

Punch Guide 48

Meet the Artists 50

Projects

Spring 18

    spring flowers, floral frames and borders, festive pots and groovy scrapbook pages

Easter 23

    decorative eggs, daisy frame, easter bonnet, borders and page ideas

Wedding 27

    wrapping paper, portrait page, beribboned frame, going-to-the-chapel hats

Baby 30

    shower invitation, birth announcement, baby pages, borders and embellishments

Hearts 34

    candy box lid, eight great uses for a heart punch, lovely valentine ideas

Quilts 36

    hanging quilt, heart-strung borders, quilt block designs and buttons

Autumn 38

    wreaths, sunflower frame, butterfly and kitchen borders, harvest and turkey ideas

Circles 42

    peacock, rope border, balls, bears, bugs and more

Animals 44

    lions, tigers, bears and many more great animal designs and borders

Contents

It's easy, creative and fun. It's punch art!

With only a handful of punches and a stack of paper, anyone can create projects that range from whimsical to stunning. All it takes is a bit of know-how and imagination. That's what makes punch art so wonderful and why many people are turning to punches when decorating scrapbook pages and embellishing invitations or stationery. But punches can be used for much more. By layering and cutting, punch artists turn ordinary shapes into projects so complex and eye-catching that they belong as featured wall hangings or illustrations in picture books.

The possibilities of punch art are endless and waiting to be explored. So get out your punches, paper and adhesives and step into the wonderful world of punch art.

Get Creative

Look at punches as the basic tools of your craft, like a painter's brushes or a sculptor's chisels. Punches help you produce the building blocks of your art project. But the real fun begins when you begin playing with the basic punched shapes. Through your choice of solid and printed papers and the way you put together the shapes, you create a unique piece of art. By layering punched pieces and adding details, for example, a daisy can grow petals and dimension that make it more interesting and realistic.

Inspiration

Art begins with inspiration. In looking for ideas for your own punch creations, browse through fabric stores, thumb through greeting card and postcard displays, look at picture books, or wander through an art gallery or zoo. Look—really *look*—at the world around you. You might find your best ideas resting in a backyard flower garden or floating overhead in a summer sky.

Theme

Punch artists often create around themes that support a design or existing photos. For example, an artist working on a spring scrapbook page might enhance it with punched flowers or baby animals, while an artist designing a fall page might scatter burnished punched leaves along its border (see page 40). Choose art for themes by asking yourself these questions: What objects traditionally represent this subject? What objects or shapes repeatedly appear in photos or paintings of this event? What objects capture the mood of the moment? What colors best portray the emotions evoked by this theme?

The Shape of Things

All things are made up of shapes. Put together in different ways, these shapes create forms. A crow, for example, has a body (an inverted heart), a head (a circle), a beak (a cut star), wings (halves of a birch leaf) and feet (cut snowflakes). As you learn to dissect the shapes of objects, you free yourself from the limitations imposed by the number of available punches. When building with basic shapes, you have more freedom to determine the style and character of the objects you portray. You can add a portion of a punched sun to a bird's head to make it a rooster, or make a bill out of a halved circle to turn your bird into a pelican. Building with shapes also lets you play with color and, in so doing, change the punched design. By making the crow (below) with brown and red paper rather than black, the bird instantly becomes a robin.

Growing With Your Art

Punch art can be as complicated as you make it. This book offers punch projects for everyone from novice to expert. Begin with one that suits your abilities. Don't be afraid to fail. If your first attempt doesn't work out, simply begin again.

You will find your enthusiasm growing right along with your confidence. Both will move forward as you gain experience and enlarge your punch collection. In the meantime, don't allow a limited number of punches to hold you back. Borrow from friends, throw a share-your-punches party, and freehand cut shapes when necessary.

This book is full of great ideas to get you started. Once you have mastered the basics, you'll find yourself substituting shapes, exploring colors and dreaming up your own designs.

The tools that make it possible!

A decade ago, the standard hand punch and a limited selection of craft punches were all that were available. Then, in the mid '90s, paper crafting took off. In response, a wider selection of punches was produced. Now they come in hundreds of designs and patterns offered in sizes from mini to jumbo. They're made for corners, borders, easy-to-reach places and those areas that need a stretch. While punch sizes and names differ slightly among manufacturers, here are the most common types.

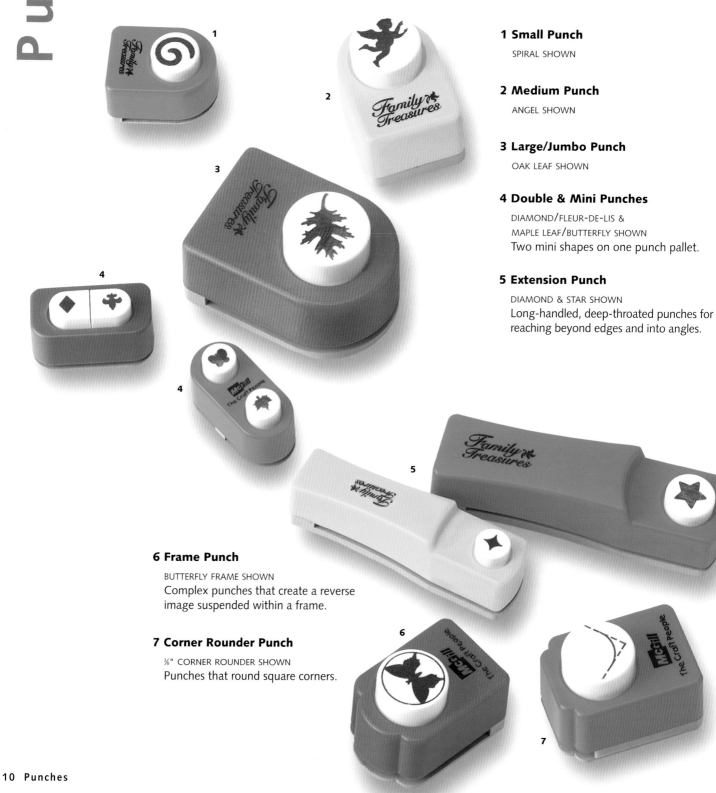

1 Small Punch
SPIRAL SHOWN

2 Medium Punch
ANGEL SHOWN

3 Large/Jumbo Punch
OAK LEAF SHOWN

4 Double & Mini Punches
DIAMOND/FLEUR-DE-LIS &
MAPLE LEAF/BUTTERFLY SHOWN
Two mini shapes on one punch pallet.

5 Extension Punch
DIAMOND & STAR SHOWN
Long-handled, deep-throated punches for reaching beyond edges and into angles.

6 Frame Punch
BUTTERFLY FRAME SHOWN
Complex punches that create a reverse image suspended within a frame.

7 Corner Rounder Punch
⅜" CORNER ROUNDER SHOWN
Punches that round square corners.

8 Corner Decoration Punch

HEART CORNER DECORATION SHOWN
Shallow punches that create patterns in corners.
Can be adjusted to allow for varying depths.

9 Decorative Corner Rounder Punch

HEART DECORATIVE CORNER ROUNDER SHOWN
Two-in-one punches that round square
corners and create a decorative corner design.

10 Corner Lace Only Punch

CORNER LACE ONLY #113 SHOWN
Punches that trim square corners into delicate,
lace-like corners.

11 Corner Lace Decorative Punch

TEARDROP CORNER LACE EDGE SHOWN
Complex punches that cut both a lace-like
corner and an elegant corner design.

12 Border/Edge Punch

SCROLL BORDER SHOWN
Punches for carving patterns along straight edges.
Can be used to create running designs.

13 Silhouette Punch

BOW SILHOUETTE SHOWN
Complex punches that create a silhouette shape with
inner punched areas.

14 Hand Punch

¼" RECTANGLE HAND PUNCH SHOWN
Simple, scissor-like punches that add delicate detail
to projects.

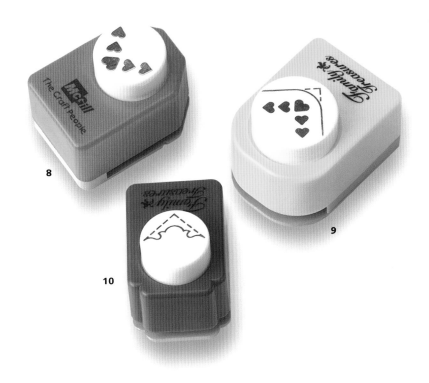

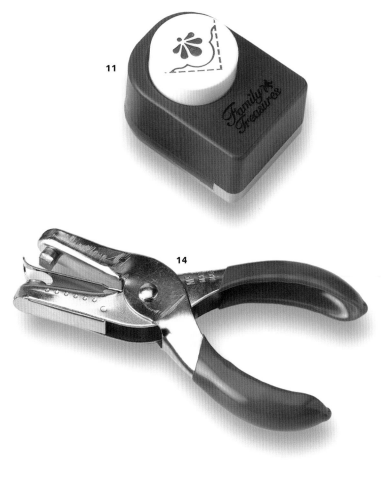

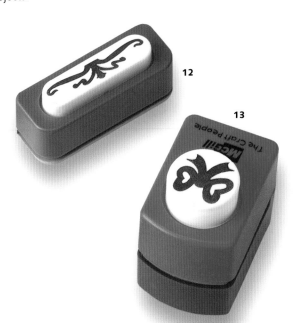

Add color, depth and texture.

Wide selections of papers now make it easier than ever for artists to bring their punch designs to life. By mixing colors, textures and weights, layered punched shapes take on dimension. The availability of hues in acid-free, lignin-free, buffered paper opens up avenues of creativity for album artists who wish to protect their photos while decorating memorable scrapbook pages. More adventuresome punch artists might wish to explore other types of paper. Here is a sampling of the many available choices.

Acid-Free and Lignin-Free Paper

Archival quality paper will not discolor over time or damage photographs. It comes in hundreds of colors and patterns. Cardstock and lighter weight papers are available in single sheets or packets. This is the best type of paper to use when working with photographs. When using these nonarchival materials, make sure they do not come in contact with a photograph.

Self-Adhesive Sticker Paper

This is a slick-faced paper with a sticky back. Just punch, peel away the protective liner, and adhere. Sold in packets, it is available in limited colors.

Photographs

Photographs lend an interesting dimension to punched shapes. Try punching leaves out of photos of real leaves or hands out of photos of hands.

Tissue Paper and Wrapping Paper

With a delicate touch, tissue paper can give punch art a gossamer effect. Before punching, sandwich two layers of tissue between sheets of a medium-weight paper. Layer tissue over other types of paper or other tissue shapes. Don't forget to consider the variety of beautiful wrapping papers.

Postcards and Greeting Cards

You'll find an assortment of colors and designs that can make a simple punched shape something dramatic. Punching heavier stock requires sharp punches and a firm hand. You might need to step gently on the punch in order to cut the shape.

Maps, Magazines and Newspapers

For truly interesting patterns, colors and pictures, recycle images from materials you're ready to throw away.

Fabric, Wallpaper, Lightweight Plastic, Vinyl and More

While many punches won't cut these durable and heavy materials, some sturdy hand punches will. So experiment. An easier solution is to color copy fabric, ribbon or other material and then punch the copy.

What holds it all together?

Just as punch and paper selections have grown in recent years, so have the adhesive options. When looking for adhesives to use on your scrapbook punch projects, be sure to look for the words *photo-safe* and *acid-free*. These products will not damage photos with which they come in contact. Beyond safety limitations, the right adhesive for you is the one that works best for your project and your budget.

Xyron 850

This machine (below) turns anything into a sticker by applying an acid-free adhesive backing to inserted paper. It also laminates. Because the Xyron adds layers of adhesive and laminate, the paper becomes more difficult to punch. Therefore, it is most appropriate for lightweight papers and is perfect for delicate work. To use the Xyron, simply insert the paper and turn the crank to apply the adhesive backing. Then punch shapes as usual. The Xyron operates without heat or chemicals, has no motor and requires no electricity or batteries. Extra adhesive cartridges are available.

Glue Markers, Glue Sticks, Glue Pens

These adhesives are available in acid-free, photo-safe products. These forms of glue applicators offer no-spill easy bonding. When working with tiny punched pieces, use applicators with fine tips.

Tape

Acid-free, heat-resistant tapes and tape-like products work well on some punched projects. Double-sided tapes come with peelable backs and can be detached in tiny pieces. A product called DryLine™, which is applied by gliding a dispenser across a page, leaves a clear adhesive strip on the paper. It is best used on larger projects or when mounting a finished design to a page.

Self-Adhesive Foam Spacers

These small square pads have adhesive on both sides. When placed under a punched shape, they help contour and add dimension to a project.

Tools that come in handy.

Punches, paper and adhesives will get you started on your punch-art projects, but the job will go more smoothly if you invest in a few additional tools. These will open up creative options and make it easier to lift and place tiny punched pieces.

Scissors

Cuticle, nail or craft scissors are necessary for precisely cutting apart punched shapes. Decorative craft scissors can add scallops, waves and other patterns to paper edges and shapes.

Tweezers

Tiny punched pieces can be difficult to lift and place. Tweezers make the job of precise placement easier.

Craft Knife

Removing the backing of peelable adhesives isn't always easy, but a craft knife can help lift the liner from the strip. This tool is also great for cutting apart punched shapes.

Pens

Details and flourishes can be added to punched designs with markers. Collect an assortment in various colors and tip styles. When working on projects for scrapbook pages, look for pigment ink pens, which are the most permanent over time.

Ruler

Today's rulers come with an assortment of decorative and straight edges. They help embellish pages and line up punches for precise placement.

Expert tips for punching.

How do I take care of my punches?

Punches are sturdy tools and will provide years of service if they receive proper care. Keep them dry to avoid rusting. Lubricate with lightweight oil (sewing-machine oil or WD-40) or by punching through waxed paper. Store in a dry place (plastic food-storage containers work well, as do fishing tackle boxes and embroidery floss boxes).

My punch won't compress.

Don't be afraid to stand up and put some weight on it. Punches are sturdier than you might think. Use the palm of your hand and push down hard on the punch button, or place the punch on the floor and step on it gently. If this doesn't work, you might be trying to punch through a material that is too thick. Consider switching to something more lightweight.

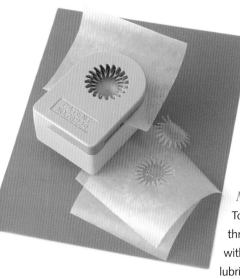

My designs seem one-dimensional.
This happens when pieces are cut from papers that are too similar in color. Create depth with patterned paper and contrasting shades.

I can't get the adhesive liner off the punched piece.
This is a job for a craft knife. Use the knife to gently pry the liner from the corners of the punched shape.

My punches stick all the time.
To prevent punches from sticking, punch regularly through standard waxed paper. Punches with chronic sticking problems may be lubricated with lightweight oil, such as sewing-machine oil or WD-40. After lubricating, be sure to punch through scrap paper several times to remove oily residue. The punches that most often stick are the more intricate designs.

I have trouble aligning border punch designs.
When trying to be precise with border alignment, it often helps to draw light guidelines on the back side of the paper. Turn the punch over and insert paper. Line up the cutting edge of the punch with the guidelines. Carefully check the alignment before punching through the paper.

When I move punched shapes around once I've adhered them, it creates a mess.
This problem can be solved by placing the completed punched shapes on the page prior to applying adhesive. Think of it as a dress rehearsal. When you're happy with the look of the design, remove the pieces and gently mark their placement with a pencil. Then adhere the pieces.

The glue turns my tiny pieces into a mess.
Smaller pieces can easily get swamped with liquid adhesive. Consider using a glue stick or pen (a less fluid adhesive), double-sided adhesive tape or paper with adhesive backing. Thinner paper can be coated with an adhesive backing using the Xyron machine. If you wish to continue working with liquid glue, try applying it with a toothpick.

The punch is stuck and I can't get my paper out.
Punches might stick when they haven't been able to complete a cut. Before you panic, try to compress the punch once more by using the methods mentioned earlier. If this doesn't work, turn the punch over. Push on a portion of the protruding punch design with a pair of scissors, a screwdriver or the handle of a spoon. This should help the punch to release. Move the punch to another section of the paper and try again. *Don't* use your fingers, the metal is sharp and you could cut yourself.

I have too many good punch-art ideas and too few punches.
Why not throw a punch party? Invite your friends (and their friends) to bring their punches and paper. You supply small resealable storage bags. Encourage your guests to stock up on punched shapes to take home and use later. Of course, you supply the cookies...and punch!

These basic techniques will get you going.

Once you've mastered five basic punch techniques, you can create thousands of punched designs.

Layering

Layering adds dimension to punched designs. By combining and positioning different punched shapes, you can create an endless number of new images.

PUNCH THE BASIC SHAPES FOR THE PIG. CUT OR TRIM PIECES AS NECESSARY. LAYER THE SHAPES STARTING WITH THE MAIN FORM.

Cutting

Cutting punched shapes makes it possible to combine paper colors and patterns for unique effects. It also allows the removal of extraneous portions of punched shapes.

PUNCH TWO BEARS OUT OF CONTRASTING PAPER. CUT AWAY TOP AND BOTTOM OF ONE BEAR SHAPE. COMBINE THE PIECES.

PUNCH THREE HEARTS FROM COMPLEMENTARY PAPERS. STACK HEARTS ON TOP OF EACH OTHER AND CUT DIAGONALLY THROUGH ALL THREE, WHICH CREATES NINE PIECES. MIX AND MATCH AS DESIRED.

Snipping

Punched shapes can be redefined by using a second punch, much as you would scissors. To create a new punched shape, simply snip away unwanted portions of the primary image with another punch.

SNIP A LG. FLOWER USING THE TEARDROP HAND PUNCH. SNIP THE STRAWBERRY USING THE SUN TO CREATE A BLUEBELL.

Negatives

Those little pieces that are left over after you have punched a silhouette or frame shape can be used for other punch designs. Layer and arrange them to add detail and dimension.

THE NEGATIVE PIECES OF FIVE PUNCHED HEART FRAMES MAKE THE STRIPES AND THE NOSE OF THE TIGER (SEE PAGE 45).

Positioning

Correct positioning of punches ensures accuracy. Incorrect positioning of punches can cause severed sides and lopsided finished projects. Begin with a sheet of paper that is slightly larger than your anticipated finished design. Always punch the smallest shape first. Flip the larger punch over, and position the punched paper into the larger punch shape. The trick is to work from the inside out.

MAKE BUTTONS OUT OF FRAME PUNCHES BY SLIPPING THE PUNCHED FRAME INTO A LG. CIRCLE PUNCH.

PUNCHES AND PUNCHED SHAPES ON THESE TWO PAGES ARE NOT SHOWN ACTUAL SIZE.

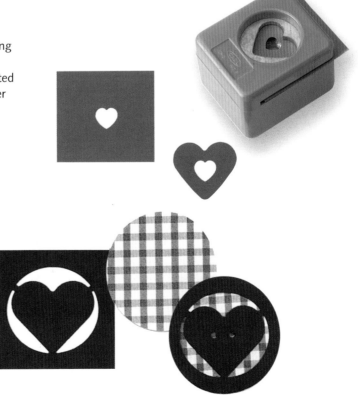

Spring

Everything's coming up roses and daffodils and tulips!
In fact, flower shapes are springing up everywhere. They're
blooming on flower pots, piled on top of yummy cones,
layered in weeping clouds and running in garden borders.
The versatile flower punch makes it all possible. So collect
your favorite punches and try these springtime projects.

Flower Pots (below)

YELLOW FLOWERS 5⁄16" and 1⁄8" round hand punches LEAVES birch leaf mini extension

BLUE FLOWERS birch leaf mini extension, dot hand punch LEAVES lg. birch leaf

Assemble flowers before attaching to pot.

Dogwood Frame

LEAVES AND FLOWERS
lg. birch leaf,
5⁄16" & 1⁄8" round hand punches,
oval hand punch
BUDS sm. egg

STEP 1 Punch leaves out of light and dark green paper. Cut light green leaves into sections. Adhere sections to dark green leaf shapes, leaving a gap so that the dark green shows through.

STEP 2 Using a semi-transparent paper and a solid color such as pink or peach, punch flower petals with the birch leaf punch and trim to smooth edges. Layer pieces of the pink petals onto transparent petals. Snip petal tips with oval hand punch.

STEP 3 Adhere flowers and leaf shapes to painted frame.

These blast-from-the-past scrapbook pages recall
the style of love beads, bell-bottoms and flower power.
While they look complicated, our groovy designs can be
easily re-created with a few cuts, slices and punches. So
collect your wildest colors and try these free-form styles.

Sixties Page

sm. circle, lg. flower, spiral, daisy silhouette

STEP 1 Use a pencil to lightly draw vertical lines about 2" apart on a piece of scrap paper. Then draw wavy vertical lines about 2" apart. Number and cut out each piece. Using the pattern as a template, cut out each piece of the checkerboard background from the desired colors. Arrange and mount on scrapbook page.

STEP 2 For shapes that will not overlap more than one color, simply punch the shape and adhere in the desired position. For shapes that overlap one or more colors, punch the entire shape out of each desired color. To piece the shape, layer punched shapes and cut straight lines first and wavy lines second, using the pattern piece to mark cutting lines.

STEP 3 Freehand cut frame and mount on page. Make a pattern for the large flower by enlarging a flower punch shape on a copy machine. Cut the flower out of two shades of paper, using one color as a mat. Adhere silhouette flower punch to center of flower and punch away center with circle punch. Accent center of flower with spiral punch.

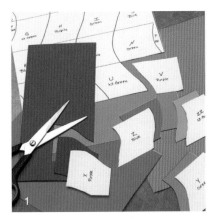

Morgan Page

sm. heart, sm circle, lg. heart, silhouette flower #2, lg. flower

STEP 1 Cut colored paper into 2" squares and mount in checkerboard pattern on page.

STEP 2 Punch flowers and hearts, using the positioning technique on page 17 for more complex designs. For shapes that overlap one or more colors, punch the entire shape out of each desired color. Layer punched shapes and cut. Mix and match halved flowers.

STEP 3 For each large daisy, punch six lg. flowers. Create petals by cutting one teardrop shape from each lg. flower. Use the sm. circle for center.

Tulip Frame Border Punch lg. tulip frame from solid paper. Turn lg. circle punch over. Slip punched tulip into lg. circle and punch to get button effect (see positioning technique on page 17). Punch another tulip frame from patterned paper. Cut flower from frame and adhere to button shape.

Wavy Flower Border sm. heart, sm. circle, sm. oval, wavy ruler

Use the large flower punch to create flowers, rain clouds, ice cream and cotton balls.

Pink Flower Snip teardrops from pe[...] edges. CENTER sm. sun, ⅛" hand punch[...]

Turquoise Flower Snip teardrops from center of top flower. CENTER flowe[...] hand punch

Blue Flower Snip teardrops from petals. CENTER flower hand punch, dot hand punch

These three flowers (left) all use the snipping technique with the teardrop hand punch, as described on page 17.

Purple Flower sm. sun, mini sun

Green Flower sm. spiral. Punch the spiral first. Then turn the flower punch upside-down and center it over the spiral (see positioning technique on page 17).

Cotton Balls Punch daisy silhouette halfway down to leave center dot intact.

Rain Clouds teardrop hand punch, sm. sun

Sunflower sm. circle, lg. birch leaf

Ice-cream Cone CHERRY sm. circle CONE sm. cross DRIPS teardrop hand punch

It's about cheeping and hopping and fluttering. It's about Easter, the holiday of rebirth. Our projects capture that special day with pastel borders, intricately decorated eggs and seasonal scrapbook pages. Get out your favorite punches and put on your Easter bonnet. It's time to start creating!

Easter Eggs

Embellish Easter eggs with whimsical punched shapes or make the delicate beauty last longer by decorating hollowed eggs.

STEP 1 Hollow out the egg shell by blowing out the contents. Begin by creating small holes in the ends of the egg with a pointed utensil. (If you experience trouble with the egg cracking, place a strip of tape over the spot prior to creating the hole. Remove the tape once the hole has been made.) While leaning over a bowl, gently blow into the hole on one end of the egg. The egg yolk and white will run out the other hole. Rinse the egg and allow to dry. Dye the eggs just as you would other Easter eggs.

STEP 2 Sandwich tissue paper between sheets of typing paper to make it easier to punch. Punch shapes such as butterflies, flowers and spirals.

STEP 3 Pour clear or white glue into a dish. Gently brush a thin layer of glue on punched tissue shape. Lay shape on egg and smooth down. It is not necessary for one punched shape to dry before layering successive shapes.

Daisy Frame daisy silhouette, sm. circle

Splashing Duck sm. umbrella BODY & HEAD sm. circle FEET & BEAK heart hand punch TAIL sm. heart. Freehand draw details.

Patchwork Border BUTTONS sm. circle EGGS lg. balloon/cut DAISY daisy silhouette, ¼" round hand punch, lg. birch leaf EGG DETAIL heart border. Freehand cut squares and draw details.

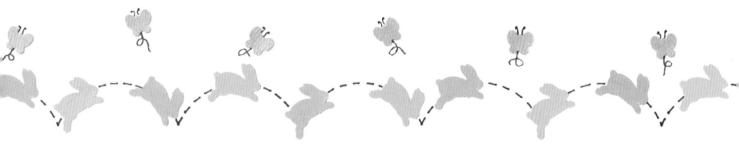

Hopping Bunny Border sm. bunny, mini butterfly. Draw dotted lines with scallop ruler.

Sun Hat HAT CROWN lg. circle HAT BRIM cut with circle template BOW lg. bow, flower hand punch LEAVES teardrop mini extension. Freehand cut hat band.

Easter Circle sm. bunny, sm. heart, heart hand punch. Lightly draw a circle using a circle template. Position bunnies and hearts along the edge.

Easter Pages

Put together a patchwork page using your favorite seasonal punches. Get creative with shapes. Let pink stars sprout from window boxes and pastel butterflies light up your borders. Or, get more complicated with funny bunnies and chirping chicks.

Flowerpot Bunny FACE lg. circle EARS lg. & med. heart/halved BOW sm. hearts CHEEKS mini heart PAWS med. heart/cut. Freehand cut pot.

Chick and Egg border
sm. egg, sm. chick. Trim edges of 1" strip of colored paper using decorative scissors. Punch shapes and back with various patterned papers.

Egg Bowl
sm. egg, sm. bow, flower hand punch BOWL lg. circle/cut and shaped. Fill with eggs punched from patterned paper.

Floral Egg
FLOWERS flower hand punch, dot hand punch, birch leaf mini extension EGG TOP & BOTTOM daisy silhouette DECORATION sm. tulip, scroll border/negative pieces EGG oval template. Layer flowers and attach leaves before adhering to egg.

Butterfly Egg
sm. dove, sm. diamond, sm. butterfly, flower hand punch, dot hand punch, mini scallop scissors SQUIGGLES country heart border/negative pieces EGG SHAPE oval template

Hen and Chicks
HEN BODY lg. balloon WING & TAIL lg. birch leaf HEAD sm. circle BEAK diamond hand punch/halved FEET star hand punch/halved CHICK BODY sm. egg WING oval hand punch TAIL oak leaf/cut HEAD ¼" round hand punch BEAK & FEET same as hen SEEDS dot hand punch. Freehand draw legs and eyes.

Spiral Border
Interlock alternating colors of punched spirals.

Splashing Ducks
(see description on page 24)

"I now pronounce you husband and wife." That was how it began... life as a married couple. Celebrate the occasion by creating beautiful mats and frames for those wedding photos. Decorate your scrapbook pages with gorgeous going-to-the-chapel hats. Wrap up gifts in elegant wrapping paper as unique as the couple who stood together and promised, "I do."

Wedding Presents

Various size heart punches, lg. birch leaf, scallop scissors, dot hand punch.
Create muted effect of large package by adhering punches directly to the gift box and wrapping with vellum paper.

Display your wedding photos or historical family wedding shots on beautiful scrapbook pages decorated with punched designs. Create this romantic photo backdrop simply by using only three punches.

Wedding Page lg. circle, sm. fleur-de-lis, diamond mini extension FLOWER Punch six fleurs-de-lis. Position in a circle around diamond. CRESCENTS Punch circle into sheet of paper. Flip punch upside down and offset previously punched circle to create a crescent-shaped piece (see picture, left). Continue cutting crescents from edge of primary circle. Position crescents in alternating directions.

Hats Our festive hats are a great way to top off any punch-art page. Call on your personal style to design just the right headwear for that special occasion. Below are the punches most often used.

HATS lg. circle, lg. rectangle, lg. balloon PURPLE HAT BRIM lg. heart PURPLE HAT FEATHER birch leaf/cut

FLOWERS flower hand punch, mini sun CENTERS ⅛" round hand punch

BOWS med. & lg. bow (consider layering ribbons), med. heart BOW KNOT & GRAPES ⅛" round hand punch RIBBON FLOURISHES scroll border/negative pieces

LEAVES birch mini extension, sm. maple

Ribbon Frame Cut paper frame. Turn filmstrip border punch upside-down and punch along edge. For even spacing, realign punch with last hole of the filmstrip. Weave ribbon over two holes and under one. Tie ends into bow.

Baby

Daniel
January 3, 1998
8 lbs. 2 oz.

Celebrate the new arrival! With a handful of punches, create
baby borders, decorations, announcements and invitations.
Make a cross-stitch sampler (above) from circles and hearts.
Like a baby, these projects are simply too sweet to be true.

Shower Invitation DUCKS sm. circle, sm. heart, mini heart, sm. bow BEAK sm. star/cut UMBRELLA Snip lg. circle with scallop punch or scissors. RAIN teardrop hand punch. Freehand draw details.

Announcement MOON lg. moon CHEEK & POMPOM ¼" round hand punch STARS & CLOUDS med., sm. & mini stars, sm. cloud HAT Use cutting technique, page 16.

Swinging on a Star MOON & STARS lg. circle/cut into crescent, sm. & mini stars HEAD & TORSO sm. circle ARM & FEET sm. oval. Freehand draw details.

Baby Bonnet BONNET & FACE lg. circle/cut BONNET RUFFLE lg. scallop CHEEK ¼" round hand punch NOSE ⅛" round hand punch RIBBONS scroll border/negative pieces. Freehand draw details.

Baby Bib BIB lg. circle NECK HOLE sm. circle. Punch sm. circle first, then position lg. circle. RUFFLE lg. scallop BLOCKS squares-triangle corner decoration/negative pieces

Jason Frame BUNNY FACE lg. & sm. circles EYES sm. oval & sm. egg NOSE mini heart EARS lg. & med. hearts/halved EMBELLISHMENTS lg., med. & sm. hearts, med. star, sm. circle

Name Border lg. bear, sm. balloon TRICYCLE sm. & mini circles SKIRT lg. scallop/cut BLANKET sm. bunny ICE CREAM flower hand punch, mini triangle. Use die cuts or freehand cut letters.

Bubbles lg. & sm. circles HIGHLIGHTS heart frame/negative pieces

Lamb Announcement sm. lamb BODY lg. scallop LEGS & FEET sm. heart FACE sm. oval STAFF sm. bow. Freehand cut and draw staff.

Rattle lg. heart, sm. circle, lg. rectangle/halved HANDLE HOLE ¼" round hand punch RIBBON scroll border/negative pieces. Freehand draw details.

mary had
a little lamb ...

McKenzie Marilyn
Jeppson
July 18th, 1998
7 lbs. 7 oz.

Buggy Babies BUGGY lg. circle/cut HEADS & WHEELS sm. circle WHEEL CENTER 5⁄16" round hand punch HANDLES sm. spiral & scroll border/negative piece HAT lg. bell/cut. Freehand draw details.

Alexandra's 1st Laugh...

She's prettier than the sweetest flower in your garden!
Display her picture on a special page. Mount strips of yellow
paper on darker paper to form the backdrop for a daisy-
strewn frame. Use a daisy silhouette punch to create the
flower shape and a 1/4" round hand punch for flower centers.

Hearts

A little heart...it's all you'll need to fashion these wonderful designs. Using positioning, snipping and layering techniques, you can create a unique candy box, decorative album pages, party invitations or a valentine for your special someone.

I love you!

Rosalyn Heart.
202 Valentine Wa
Loveland, CO 806

The large heart punch is the basic shape used to create the projects on this page.

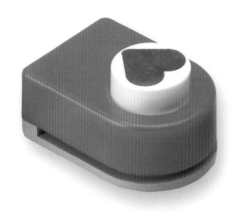

Tumbling Hearts
Using various punches, you can create endless heart designs. To make these hearts, use the positioning technique described on page 17. Remember to work from the inside out.

Rooster COMB sm. sun/halved HEAD sm. circle FEET sm. snowflake/cut BEAK sm. star/cut WINGS lg. birch leaf/halved

Mice BODY lg. heart/cut TAIL spiral EARS sm. circle NOSE & EYE ⅛" round hand punch

Butterfly BODY lg. heart/top portion

Pansies various size hearts/layered, flower hand punch

Pumpkins mini maple leaf. Freehand cut stems.

Angel HALO & HEAD sm. circle WINGS lg. scallop TORSO sm. heart

Flying Heart lg. birch leaf/halved

Quilts

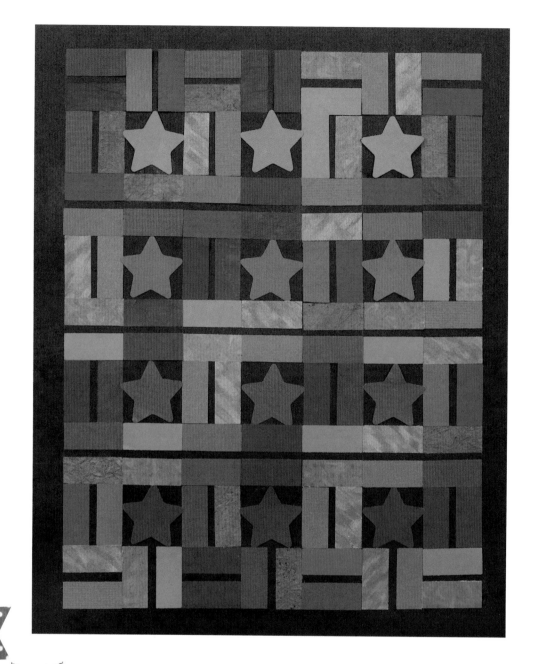

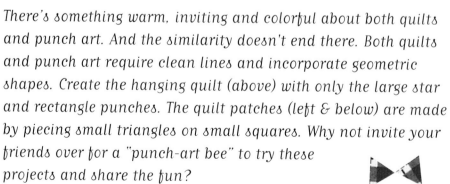

There's something warm, inviting and colorful about both quilts and punch art. And the similarity doesn't end there. Both quilts and punch art require clean lines and incorporate geometric shapes. Create the hanging quilt (above) with only the large star and rectangle punches. The quilt patches (left & below) are made by piecing small triangles on small squares. Why not invite your friends over for a "punch-art bee" to try these projects and share the fun?

Heart Swag scroll border/negative piece, sm. heart

Heart Garland lg. heart (see cutting technique on page 16)

Quilt Blocks

1 RINGS lg. circle CENTER sm. circle. Punch center from lg. circle. Slice circles and intertwine.

2 STAR-SPANGLED FLOWER med. heart, diamond mini extension

3 BLUE AND RED FLOWER lg. flower/sectioned

4 TEMPLE STAR sm. diamond/cut, lg. circle

5 DIAMOND QUILT diamond mini extension. Piece tip-to-tip.

6 STAR sm. diamond

7 HEART SQUARE sm. heart, diamond mini extension

Buttons bow, star & heart frames, lg. circle, dot hand punch (see positioning technique on page 17)

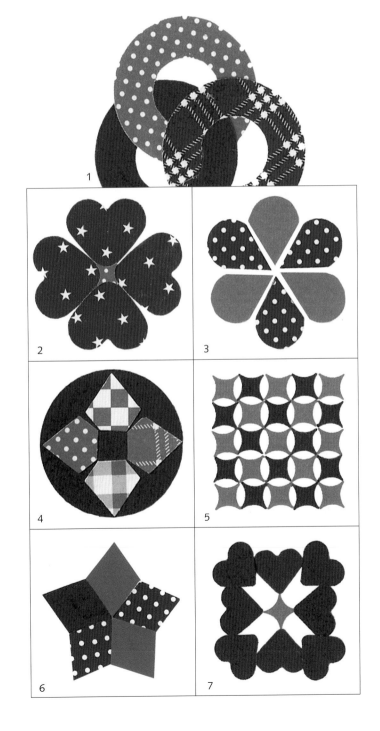

There's a nip in the air. You're in the mood for sweet apples, pumpkin harvests and Thanksgiving turkey. Indulge your fall fever with wonderful punch projects. Create this decorative shadow box by punching small circles and large leaves. Gently round "grapes" by rotating a pencil eraser in the center of the paper. Mount the grape bunch on foam core to give it more dimension.

Autumn Swag lg. maple leaf, lg. oak leaf ACORN sm. egg, large bell/cut BERRIES ⅛" round hand punch RIBBON lg. bow TWIGS scroll border/negative pieces

Heart Wreath FLOWER & BUDS silhouette flower #2 LEAVES lg. maple & birch leaf STEM sm. spiral, heart template. Draw and cut two overlapping hearts using the template. Layer flowers and leaves along border.

Sunflower Frame lg. sun, sm. circle, lg. birch leaf. Layer several punched suns and gently curl petals outward. HAT (see hats on page 29)

Butterfly Border Punch butterfly frame. Turn lg. circle punch upside-down. Slip punched butterfly into lg. circle and punch again to get button effect (see positioning technique on page 17). Punch lg. circle out of contrasting paper for backing.

Fall Leaves Page Bring back those crisp fall days with joyful scrapbook pages. Using oak, birch and maple punches in various sizes, accent photos with foliage so real you can hear the crunching leaves.

Cornstalks LEAVES lg. circle/sliced (as described in pumpkin instructions below) GRAIN heart border/negative pieces. Freehand cut stalks.

Pumpkins LARGE PUMPKINS Punch lg. circle from sheet of paper. Flip punch upside-down and offset previously punched circle to create a crescent-shaped piece of paper (see "Wedding Page" instructions on page 29). Continue punching crescents from edge of primary circle. Repeat with other shades of paper. Adhere crescent segments on darker piece of paper. Cut around completed pumpkin. Freehand cut stems. SMALL PUMPKINS Using the sm. egg shape instead of a circle, complete the design as described above.

Turkey (left) TAIL FEATHERS, BODY & WING lg. circle/cut HEAD & FEET sm. egg/halved for feet WATTLE & BEAK teardrop hand punch. Cut legs freehand.

Turkey (right) TAIL FEATHERS & WING lg. birch leaf BODY lg. circle NECK sm. heart HEAD sm. oval BEAK teardrop hand punch WATTLE swan/cut. Freehand cut feet.

Apple Barrel BARREL & SIGN med. rectangle APPLES med. apple/layered LEAVES lg. birch leaf/cut. Freehand draw details.

Kitchen Border CHERRIES ⅛" round hand punch LEAVES birch leaf mini extension BRANCH Cut freehand. ROLLING PIN med. rectangle, teardrop hand punch BOWL lg. circle/cut FLOUR BAG lg. house/cut, sm. triangle, teardrop hand punch CUP Christmas ornament silhouette/cut SPOON oval hand punch, med. rectangle/cut PIE lg. scallop, lg. heart, mini heart PIE DISH lg. heart/cut

Round and round and round it goes, and when it stops—you'll be making marvelous things! It's hard to believe that the images on this page, inspired by author Ed Emberley's wonderful book "Picture Pie: A Circle Drawing Book," and all the projects in this section are made from circles! To re-create the peacock, use a circle template for the body. Sections of large and small circles make the tail feathers and wings. A teardrop hand punch makes the eye and a mini sun decorates feather tips. Create a rope border (below) with quartered circles.

Bears MUZZLE sm. circle MOUTH oval hand punch EARS & EYES 5⁄16" round hand punch PUPILS & NOSE 1⁄8" round hand punch

Fish BODY, TAIL & FINS circles/cut EYE 5⁄16" & 1⁄4" round hand punches

Pizza PEPPERONI 5⁄16" round hand punch OLIVES oval hand punch

The large circle punch is the basic shape used to create all the projects on this page.

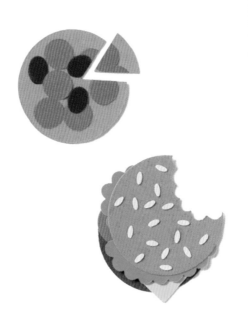

Burger LETTUCE & BITE lg. scallop SEEDS heart border/negative pieces TOMATO 5⁄16" round hand punch CHESSE sm. square

Ladybugs HEAD sm. circle DOTS 1⁄8" round hand punch

Balls BOWLING BALL 1⁄8" round hand punch. Freehand draw ball details.

Fruit RINDS lg. circle sections (see instructions for "Wedding Page" on page 29) SEEDS teardrop hand punch

Animals

Roar. Rrrbit. Squeak. A zoo full of animals springs to life with the snap of a punch. Whether you're a large cat lover or a tiny mouse aficionado, your heart will go out to our punch-art animal friends. All these furry creatures grow from basic punch shapes. It's how the pieces are combined that gives the animals their character and personalities.

Elephant, Giraffe & Lion (bottom left)
All begin with a lg. circle punch. The eyes are made with a sm. egg punch, ⁵⁄₁₆", ¼" & ⅛" round hand punches.

ELEPHANT EARS lg. and med. hearts. Freehand cut trunk.

GIRAFFE EARS sm. egg SPOTS sm. cloud HORN TIPS heart hand punch. Freehand cut mane.

LION MANE lg. sun/layered CHEEKS sm. circle EARS & NOSE ⁵⁄₁₆" & ¼" round hand punches LASHES mini sun MOUTH mini moon

Snack boxes lg. rectangle/cut POPCORN sm. cloud PEANUTS sm. butterfly/halved

Lion (left) FACE lg. circle MANE lg. flower/layered CHEEKS, NOSE & EARS sm. circle MOUTH ⁵⁄₁₆" round hand punch EYE ⅛" round hand punch WHISKERS scroll border/negative pieces

Mice BODY lg. heart/halved HEAD med. heart/halved NOSE ¼" round hand punch EARS sm. circle TAIL sm. spiral FEET sm. maple leaf/cut EYES dot mini extension CHEESE lg. heart/halved, various round hand punches

Frog BODY lg. circle LEGS & LILY PAD lg. heart/halved for knees FEET sm. heart EYES sm. circles PUPILS ⁵⁄₁₆" round hand punch

Worm & Apple APPLE lg. heart, ⁵⁄₁₆" round hand punch LEAF lg. birch leaf WORM ⁵⁄₁₆" & ¼" round hand punches

Snail mini butterfly, spiral, lg. bell/cut

Penguins sm. bow, sm. tulip BODY lg. circle WINGS lg. heart/halved HEAD med. heart/halved HAT sm. triangle, mini sun EYE dot mini extension FEET heart frame/negative pieces

Bears lg. bear/layered

Tiger HEAD lg. circle MOUTH crescent hand punch MUZZLE & EARS sm. circle STRIPES/CROWN/NOSE heart silhouette/negative pieces LASHES mini sun EYES sm. oval, ⁵⁄₁₆" round hand punch, teardrop hand punch, dot hand punch EARS sm. circle

Cat HEAD lg. circle MOUTH small moon MUZZLE sm. circle EARS sm. heart LASHES mini sun/cut STRIPES/CROWN/NOSE heart silhouette/negative pieces

Owl BODY lg. heart HEAD sm. circle WINGS med. heart/halved FEATHERS teardrop hand punch BREAST FEATHERS sm. maple leaf FEET heart frame/negative piece LASHES mini sun/halved BEAK mini star/cut

All our bouncing bears are made with the medium bear punch.

BOTTLE BEAR silhouette baby bottle

EASTER BEAR sm. bow, sm. heart/halved

BABY BEAR tiny bear, sm. bow

LOVE BEARS heart hand punch BUBBLE lg. scallop, ⅛" round hand punch

APPLE BEAR mini apple TREE lg. tree, apple corner punch/negative pieces

PARTY BEAR sm. balloon, sm. cake/layered

COWBOY BEAR sm. heart/cut, spiral

BEACH BEAR sm. heart/cut

IRISH BEAR sm. shamrock, birch mini extension, ⅛" round hand punch HAT sm. heart

ARTIST BEAR PALLET sm. egg. Freehand cut hat and paintbrush.

Peacock BODY & HEAD lg. & med. hearts/halved FAN FEATHERS lg. & sm. suns/layered FEATHER CORE (red) lg. & med. circles, ¼" round hand punch BODY PLUMAGE, EYE & BEAK teardrop hand punch/halved for the beak RUFF sm. sun/cut FEET sm. musical note/cut PUPIL dot hand punch

Fire Hydrant lg. bell/cut, sm. dog, mini maple leaf

Farm Scene sm. animal punches SILO lg. bell/cut, sm. & mini squares HAY mini maple leaf. Freehand cut hills.

46 Animals

Instructions for art on general pages.

FLOWERS/TITLE PAGE lg. birch, star frame/ snipped, sm. sun, diamond mini extension

WHEAT/LETTER FROM PUBLISHER GRAIN teardrop mini extension, daisy silhouette/petals. Freehand cut stems. BUG HEAD 5⁄16" round hand punch BODY sm. egg WINGS sm. heart/halved LEG country heart border/negative pieces

CIRCLES/CREDITS PAGE

SPRING CIRCLE FLOWERS 1⁄8" round & dot hand punches, mini fleur-de-lis/cut, teardrop hand punch, sm. tulip, flower & star hand punches BIRD sm. dove. Freehand cut leaves, stalks and circle.

FALL CIRCLE CORNUCOPIA lg. circle/cut, lg. scallop, sm. apple, apple corner decoration/ negative pieces RED FLOWERS mini sun, 1⁄8" round hand punch SUNFLOWERS lg. sun, sm. circle GRAPES 1⁄8" round hand punch, mini maple leaf WHEAT heart and teardrop border/negative pieces

PUNCH FAIR SUNFLOWERS lg. sun, sm. circle, lg. birch leaf DAISIES daisy sihouette, 5⁄16" round hand punch LEAVES sm. balloon HOLLYHOCKS sm. shamrock, 1⁄8" round hand punch IRIS fleur-de-lis/cut, teardrop hand punch POTS med. rectangle, lg. bell GRASS sm. sun BANNER freehand cut sign, lg. & sm. hearts RIBBONS scroll border/negative pieces

SUNFLOWER/TABLE OF CONTENTS lg. sun, daisy silhouette, lg. circle OUTER PETALS lg. flower (cut petals as described on page 21)

NOAH'S ARK PG. 9 sm. & mini animals BOAT med. rectangle, sm. house, lg. circle/cut

SPRING SCENE PG. 18 HYDRANGEAS heart hand punch, lg. birch leaf & 1⁄8" round hand punch ASTERS lg. & sm. sun, flower hand punch TULIPS lg. balloons & oval hand punch DAFFODILS lg. old tree/cut, sm. sun, sm. oval LUPINES oval hand punch, 1⁄8" hand punch, sm. oval, sm. eggs BEE sm. egg, sm. circle, oval hand punch. Freehand cut stalks.

BIRDHOUSES PG. 47 lg. bell, lg. house, med. tree, med. rectangle, sm. bell, hearts of different sizes, 1⁄4" round & dot hand punches, triangle hand punch, sm. dove, sm. and mini maple leaves

FINGER PUPPETS/MEET THE ARTISTS lg. hand punch, various sm. animal punches

Thanks to the following manufacturers whose products helped make this book possible.

PUNCHES

All Night Media® Inc.
Box 10607, San Rafael, CA 94912

Family Treasures
24922 Anza Ave. Unit D, Valencia, CA 91355

Marvy Uchida
3535 Del Amo Blvd., Torrance, CA 90503

McGill, Inc.
131 E. Prairie St., Marengo, IL 60152

PAPER

Canson-Talens, Inc.
21 Industrial Dr., South Hadley, MA 01075

The Paper Patch
P.O. Box 414, Riverton, UT 84065

Paper Garden
3317 E. Russell Rd., Las Vegas, NV 89120

ADHESIVES

American Tombow, Inc. (Mono®Aqua)
4467-C Park Dr., Norcross, GA 30093

EK Success (2 Way Glue Pen)
P.O. Box 6507, Carlstadt, NJ 07072

Gilette (DryLine™ adhesive)
Boston, MA

Xyron
14698 No. 78th Way, Scottsdale, AZ 85260

PENS

Sakura of America
30780 San Clemente St., Hayward, CA 94544-7131

SCISSORS

Fiskars®, Inc.
7811 W. Stewart, Wausau, WI 54401

Picture Pie: A Circle Drawing Book by Ed Emberley ©1984 Little, Brown and Company, Boston, MA

Punch Guide

Commonly Used Punches

The punch shapes below are some of the ones used most frequently throughout this book and are shown for your reference. Not all punches used are shown. Punch shapes are displayed at 100%.

Mini Punches

BIRCH LEAF	BUTTERFLY	DIAMOND	HEART
OAK LEAF	STAR	SUN	TEARDROP

Hand Punches

5/16" ROUND	1/4" ROUND	1/8" ROUND	DOT/1/16" ROUND
HEART	FLOWER	OVAL	TEARDROP

Frame Punches

BUTTERFLY FRAME PUNCH

HEART FRAME PUNCH

TULIP FRAME PUNCH

Small Punches

 CIRCLE

 EGG

 OVAL

 DIAMOND

 SQUARE

 TRIANGLE

STAR

 HEART

SUN

 CLOUD

MAPLE LEAF

 OAK LEAF

SNOWFLAKE

TULIP

STRAWBERRY

FLEUR-DE-LIS

 BELL

 BOW

 BALLOON

 SPIRAL

Border Punches

COUNTRY HEART

HEART

SCROLL

Large Punches

CIRCLE   HEART   FLOWER

BIRCH LEAF   MAPLE LEAF   OAK LEAF

Animals

DOVE   SMALL BEAR

BUNNY

BUTTERFLY   MEDIUM BEAR

SUN   MOON   SCALLOP

LAMB   LARGE BEAR

BALLOON   BELL   BOW

Medium Punches

APPLE   HEART   RECTANGLE   STAR   TREE

left to right
Erica Pierovich, Joyce Feil (contributing artist),
Tonya Jeppson and Pam Klassen

Paper crackled. Punches snapped. Laughter and conversation flew when the artists met at the Satellite Press corporate office to dream up and create the delicious ideas within this book. You're familiar with their work. Now, meet the artists...

Tonya Jeppson

"I love punches! Unlike stickers, you can use them over and over again and manipulate the pictures until you've got just the effect you want," says Tonya, an Idaho-based scrapbook instructor. She draws punch-art ideas from her woodworking, painting and cross-stitch projects. How does this busy wife and mother find time for all her projects? "My girls sit next to me and work on their projects while I work on mine. Kids love punches, too!"

Pam Klassen

"Before having the opportunity to work with punches, I thought of them as limited. I didn't see the potential for designs beyond the punches' dedicated use. Now, I wonder how I could have overlooked all the possibilities!" says Pam, a devoted scrapbook artist. She and her husband, a ranch manager, live in Springdale, Utah. They have just celebrated the birth of their first child. Will punch art find a place in their daughter's album? You bet!

Erica Pierovich

"I love punch art because it gives me enormous control over color, style and texture. I can blend the artwork much easier than working with stickers," says Erica, a Longmont, Colorado computer systems manager. Erica discovered punch art a year ago when first introduced to scrapbooking. Having inherited few photos of her own youth, she's determined to document the memories of childhood for her kids. She says punch art helps make her album pages as unique as the experiences recorded there.